Caddo Lake

water, light and atmosphere

by Duane Johnson

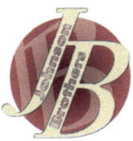

Copyright © 2010 by Duane Johnson

First Edition

International Standard Book Number:

1450508979

Published by Johnson Brothers Productions

Printed in the United States of America

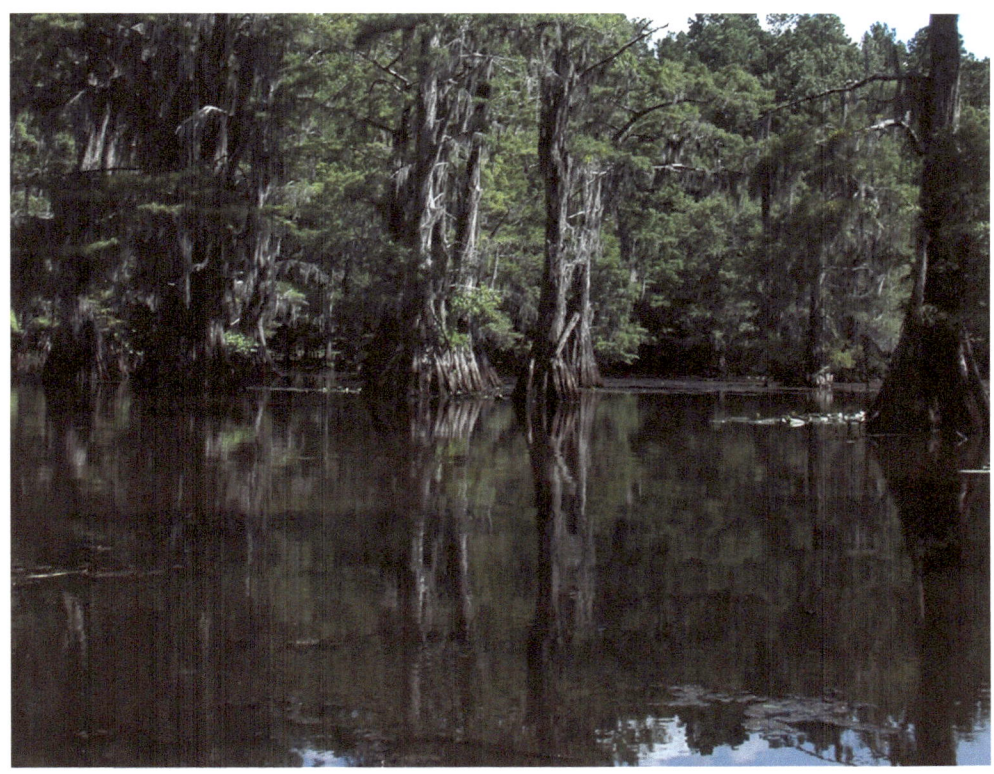

Caddo Lake is a lake and wetland located on the border between Texas and Louisiana, in Northern Harrison County and Southern Marion County in Texas and western Caddo Parish in Louisiana. It is an internationally protected wetland under the RAMSAR treaty and is the largest natural fresh water lake in the South, and the largest Cypress forest in the world.

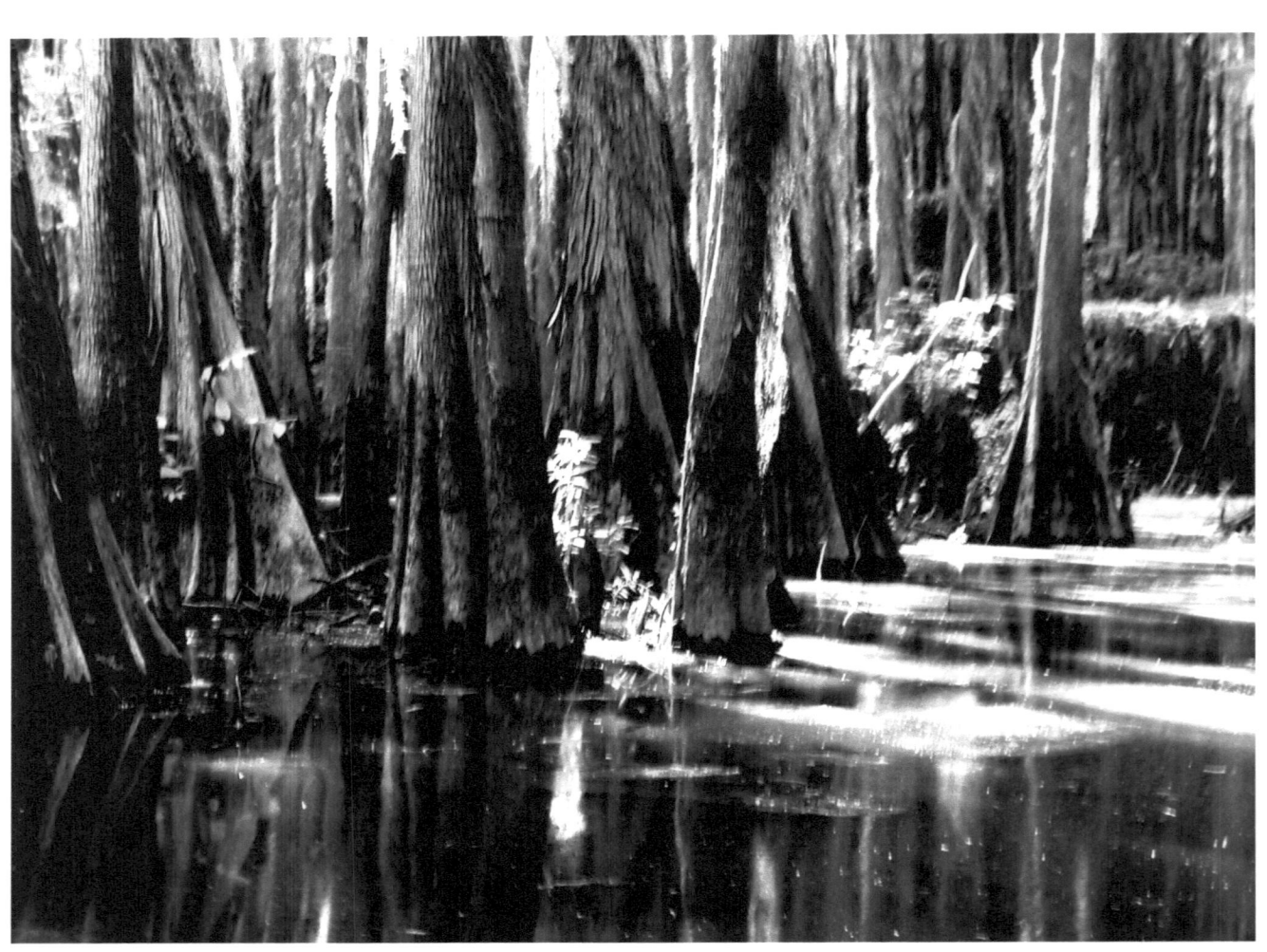

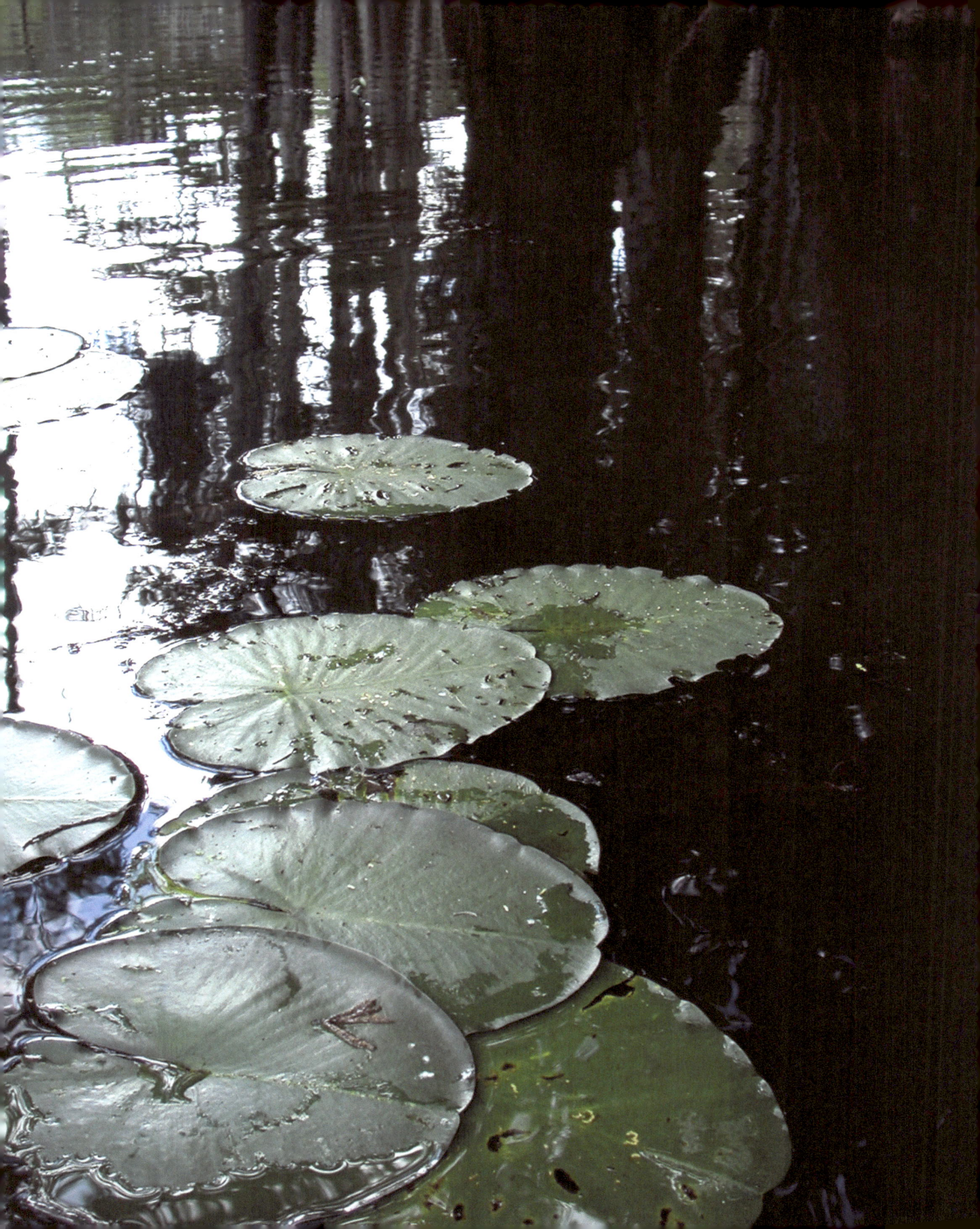

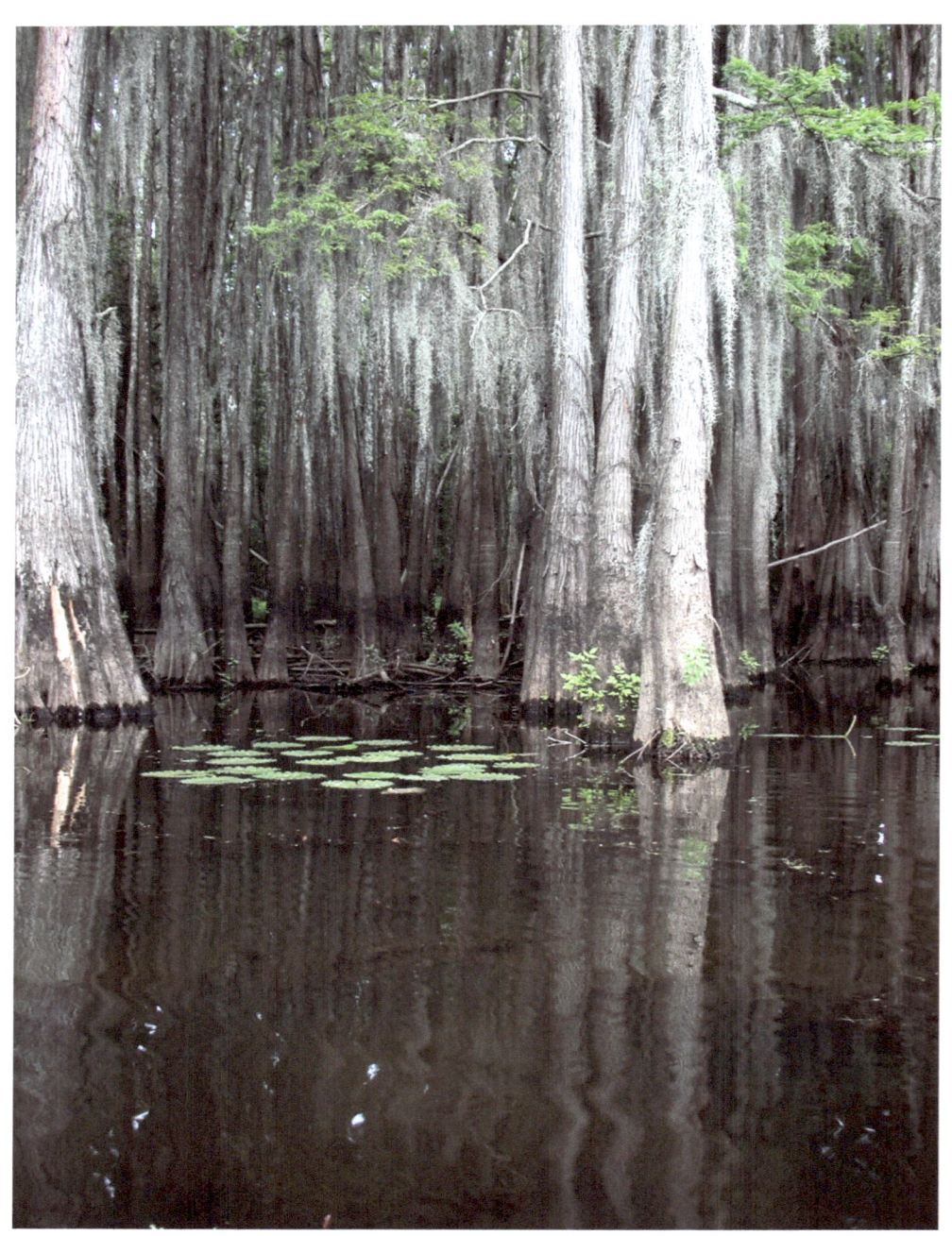

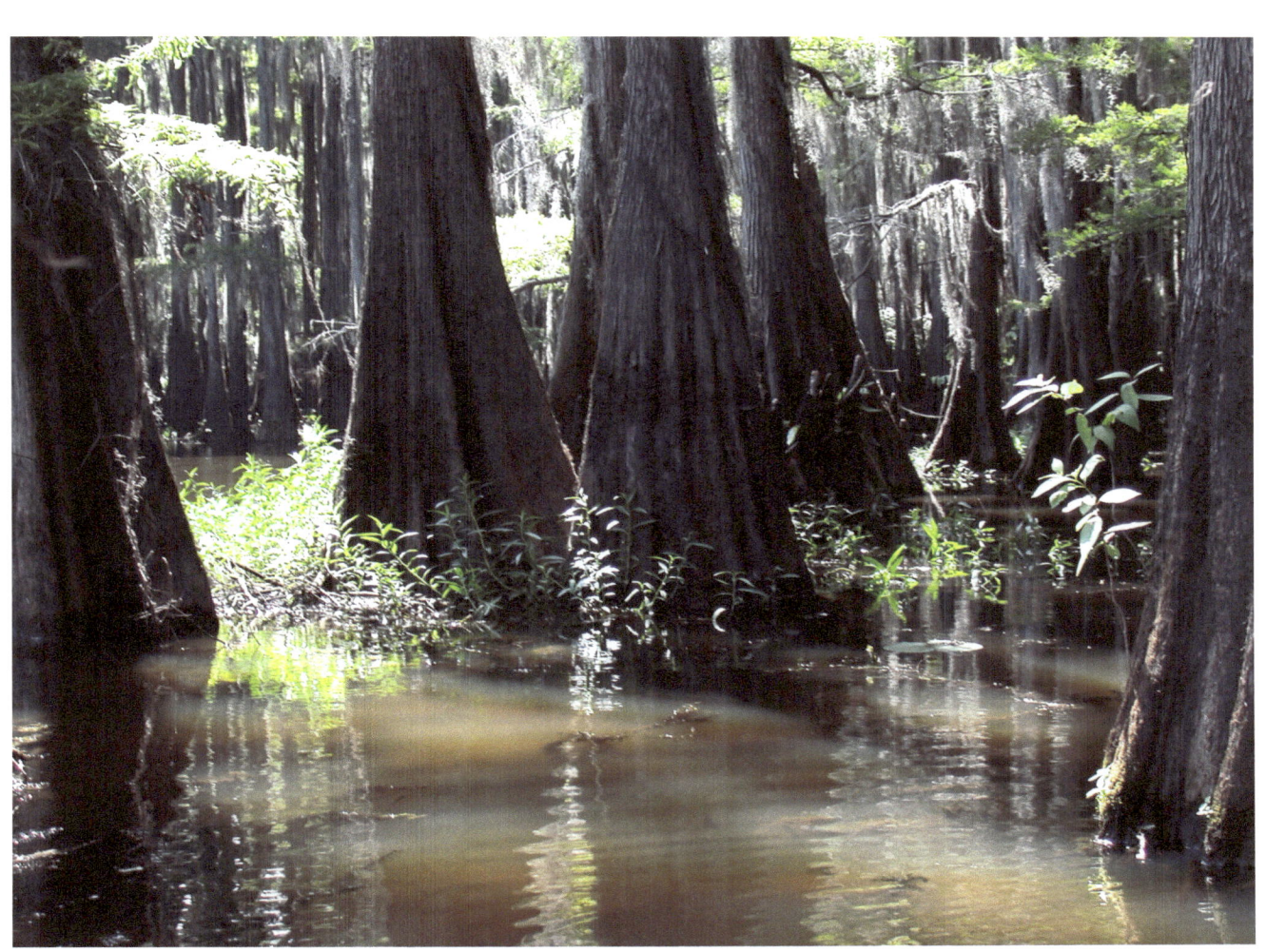

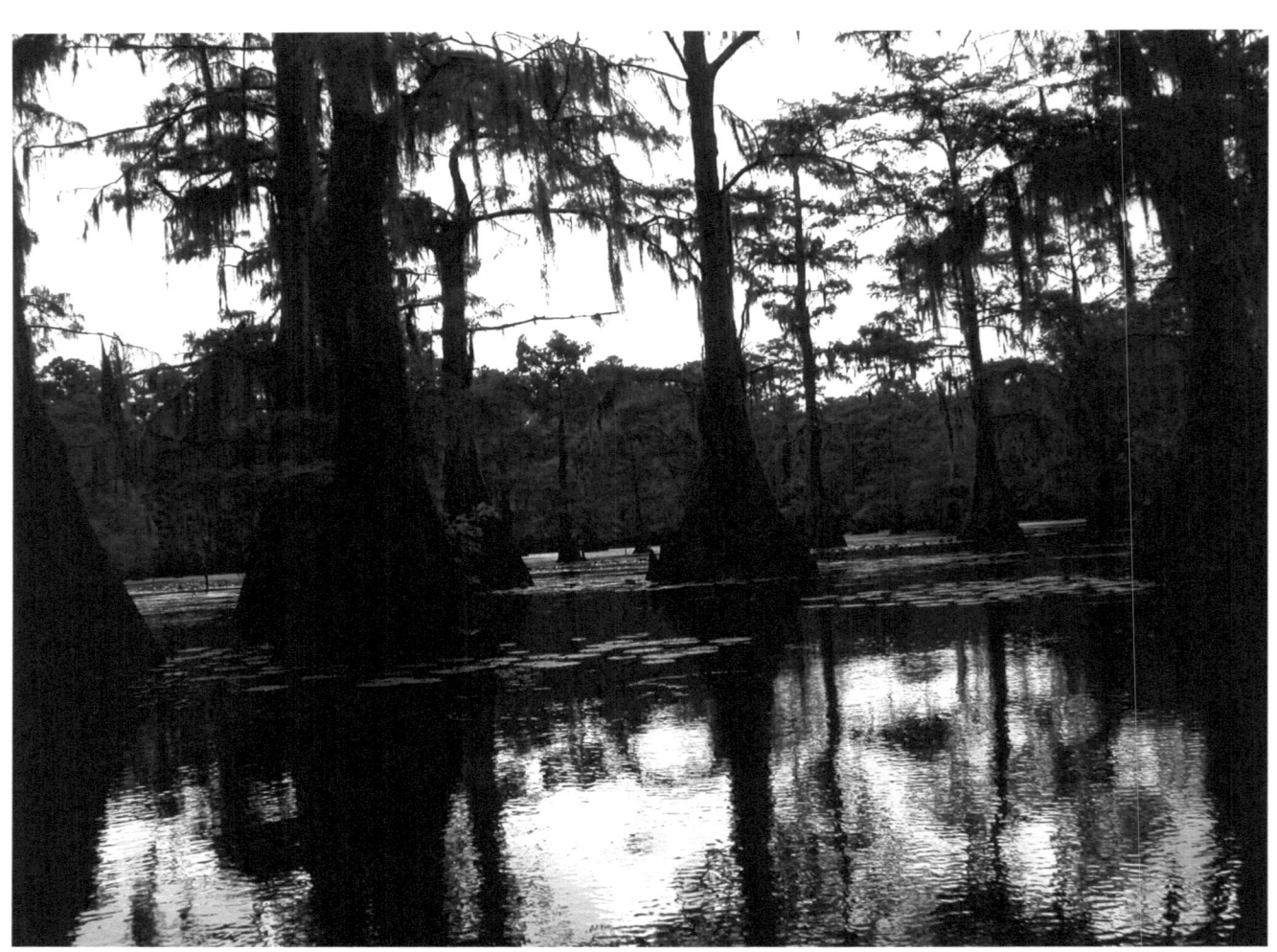

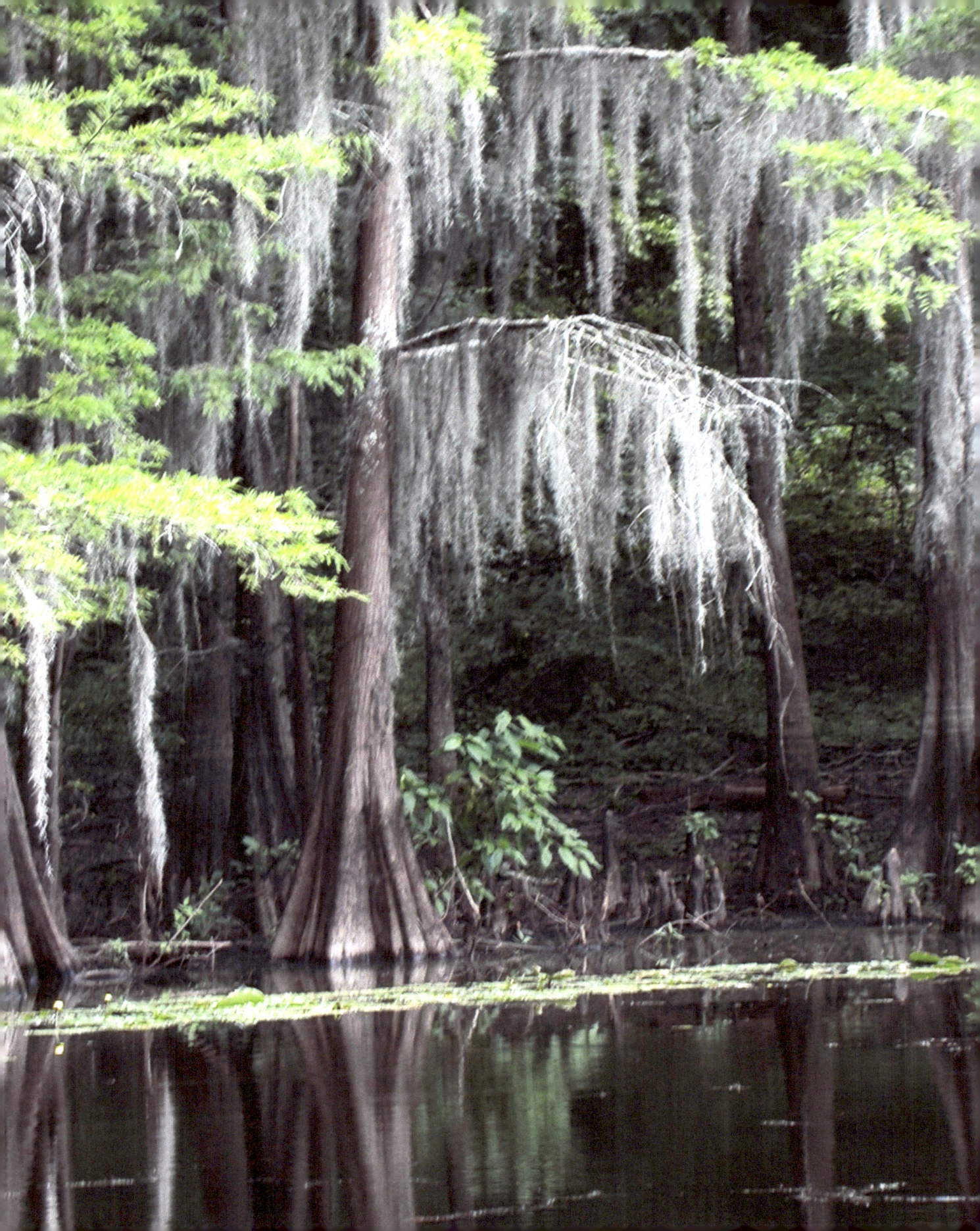

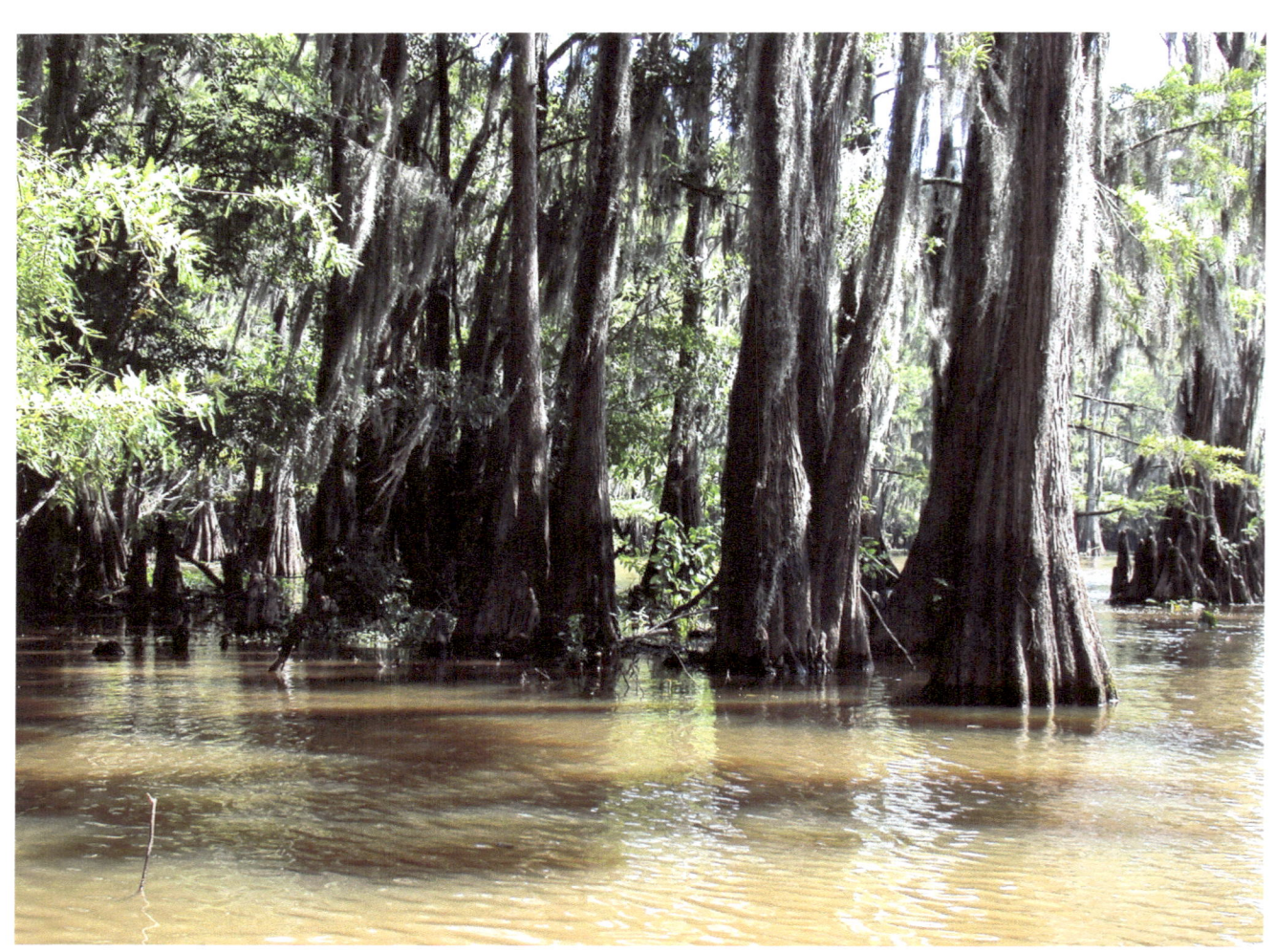

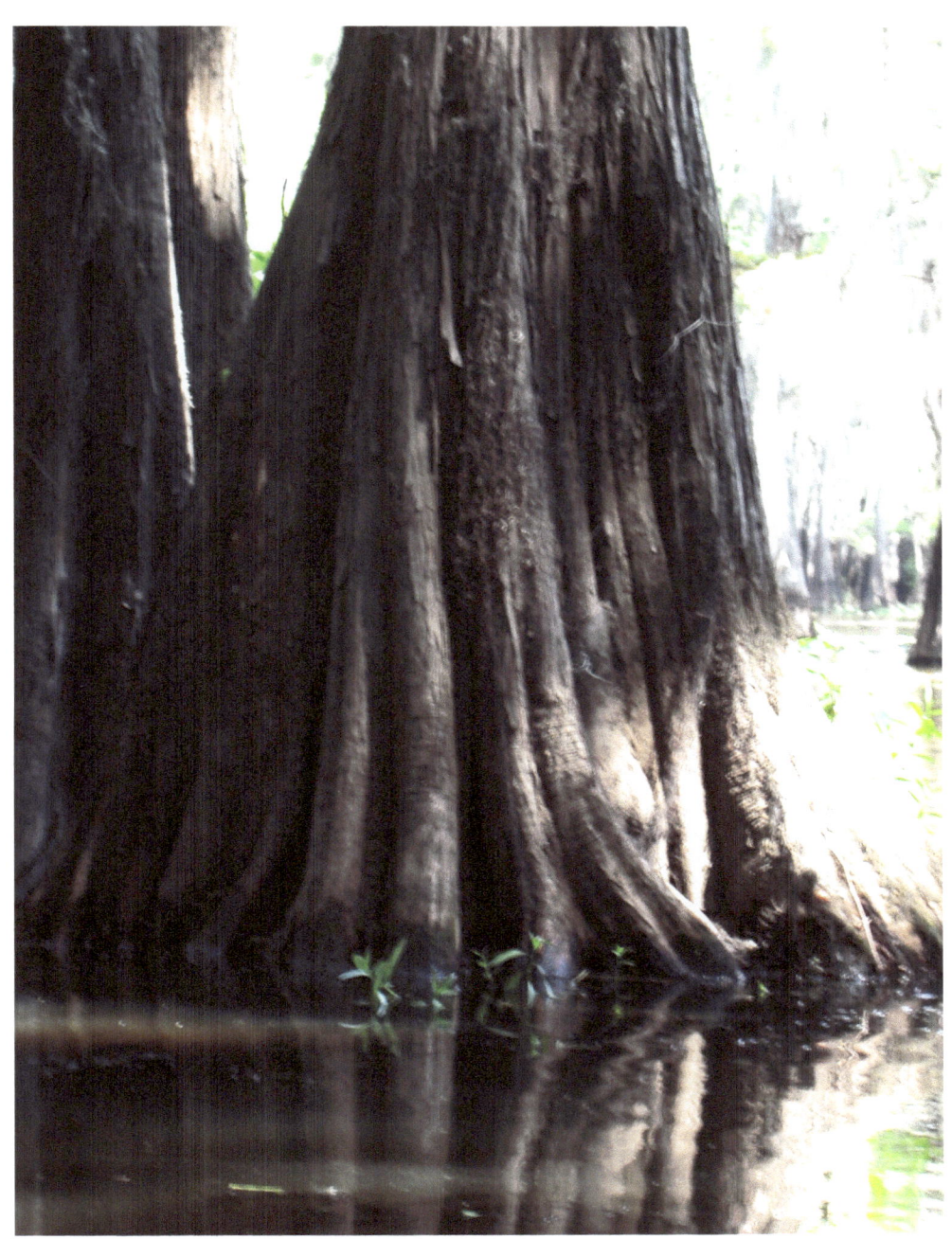

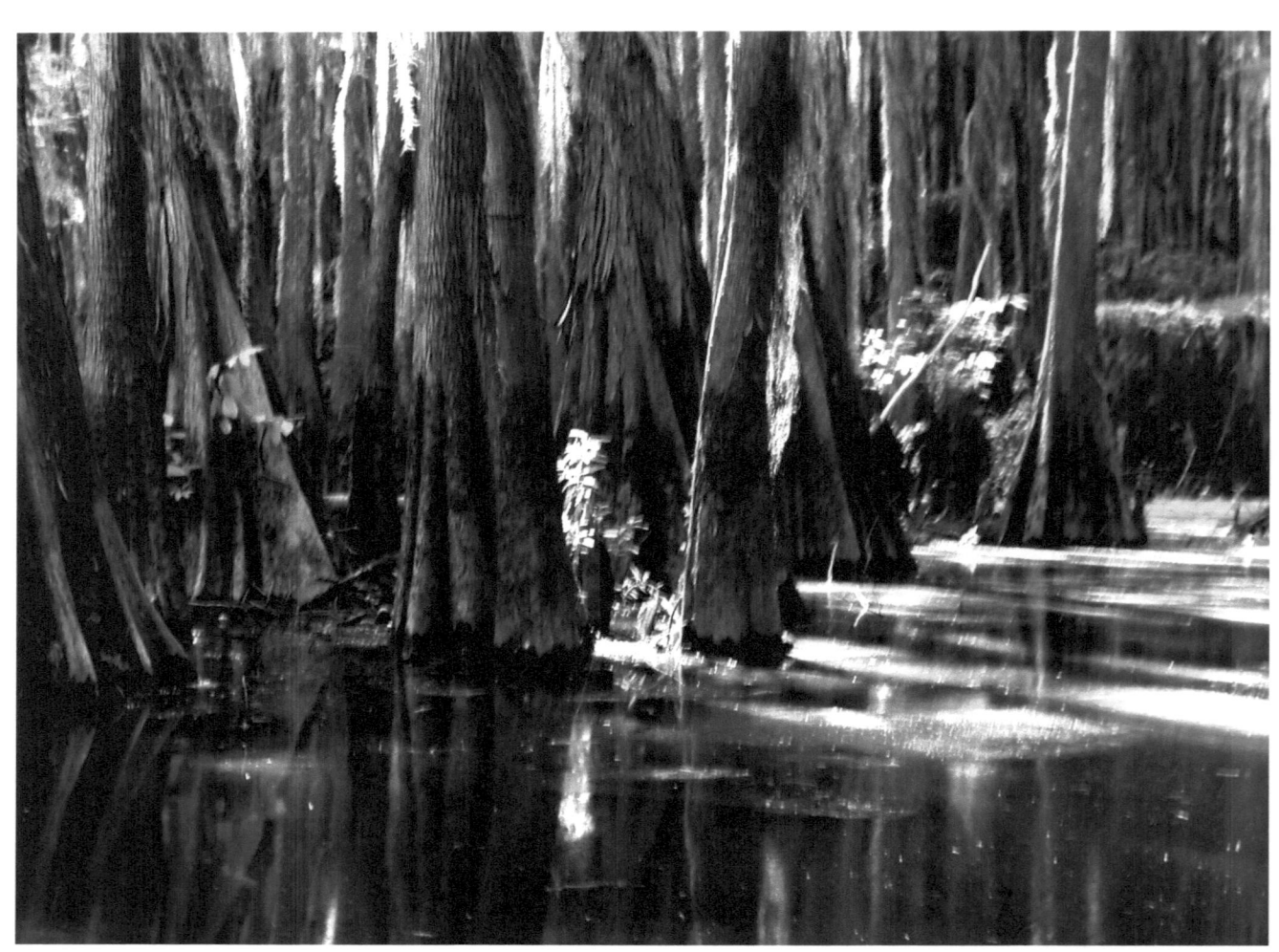

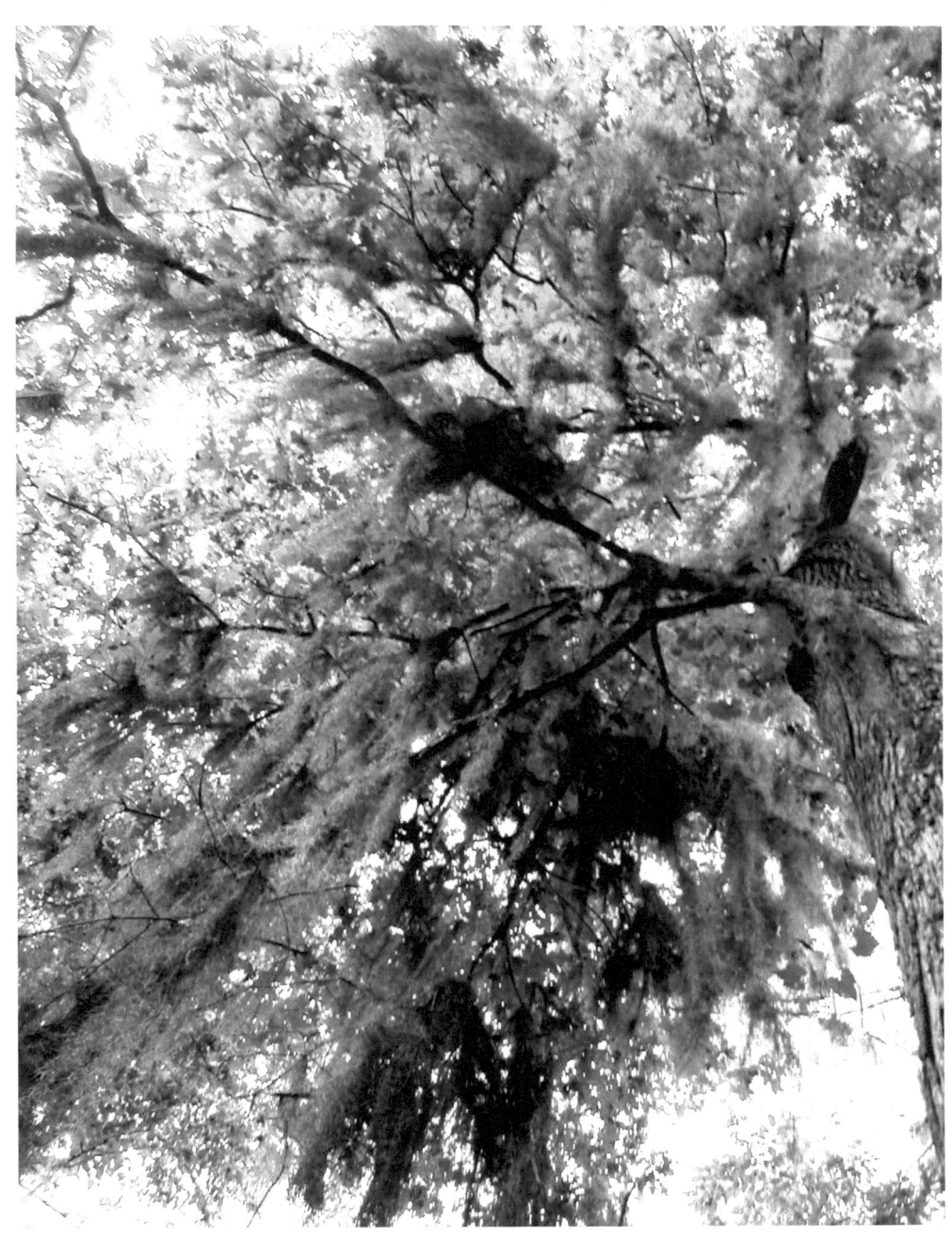

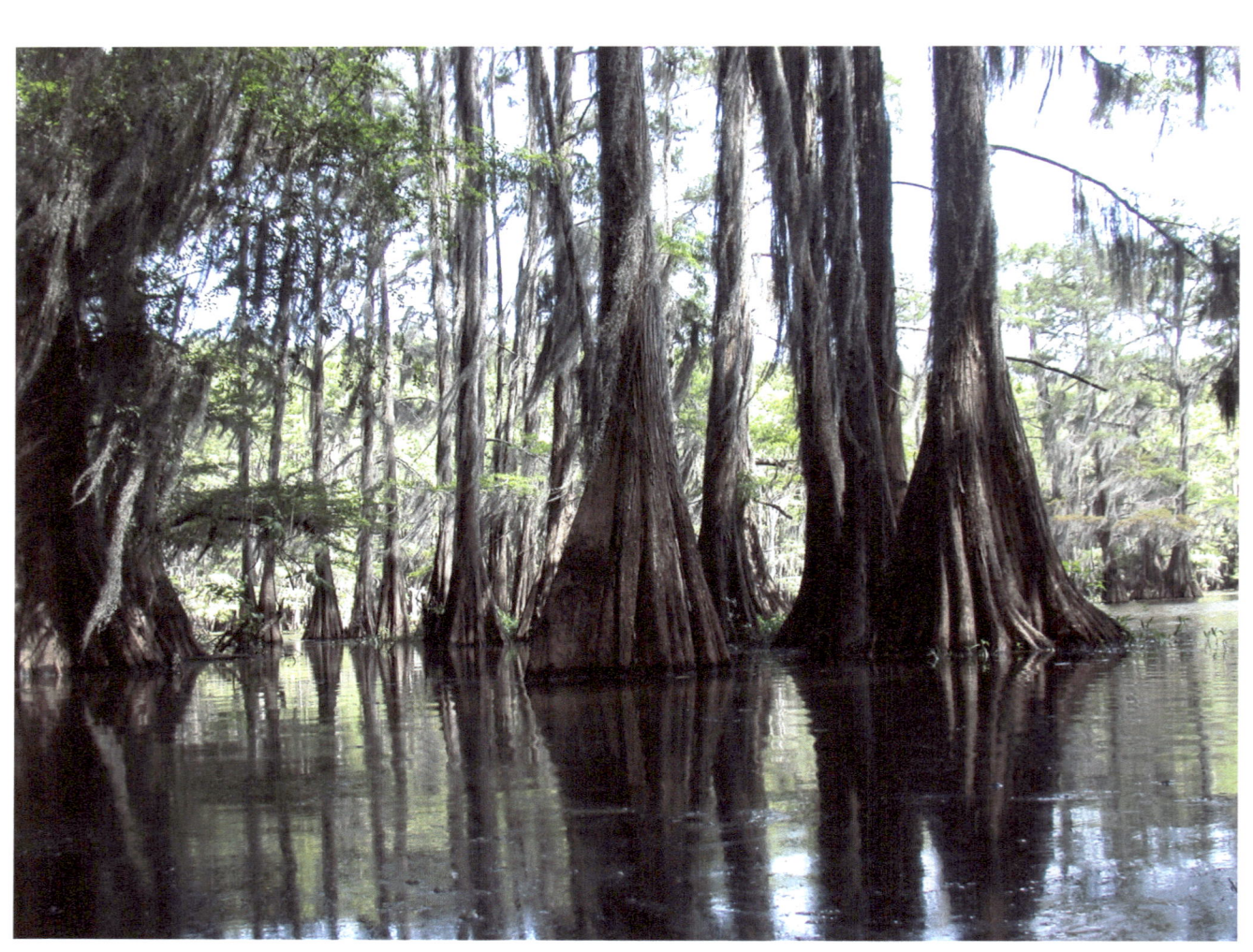

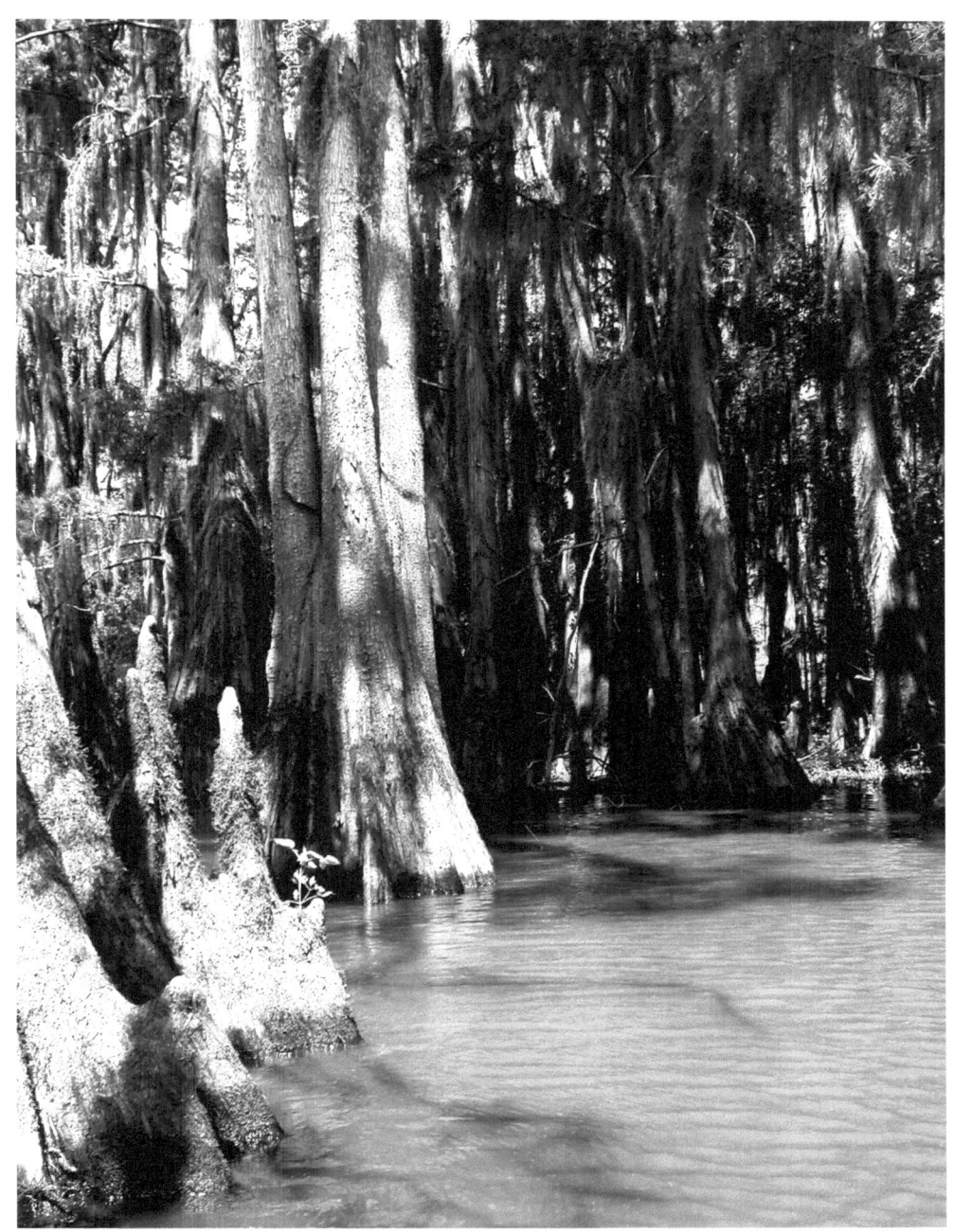

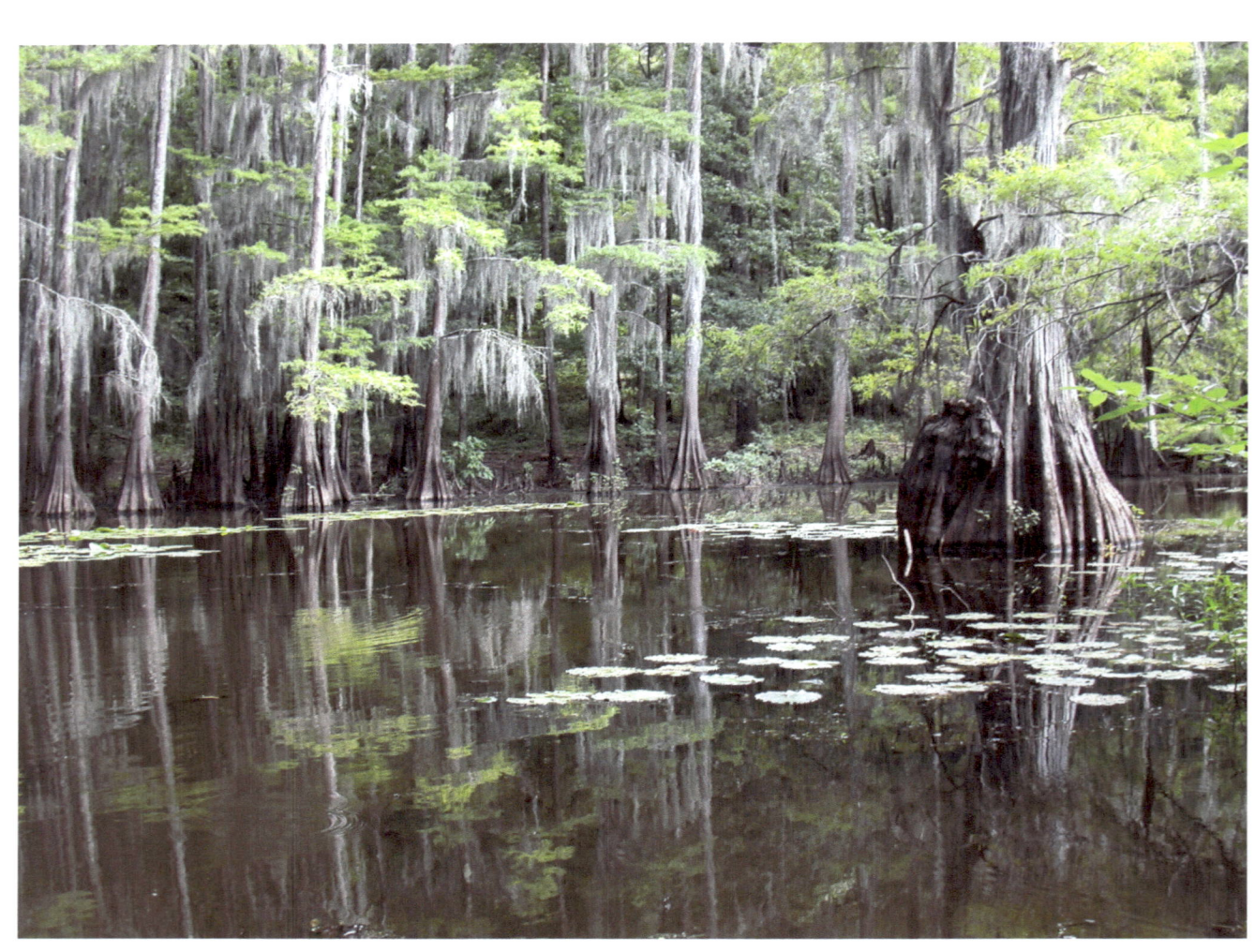

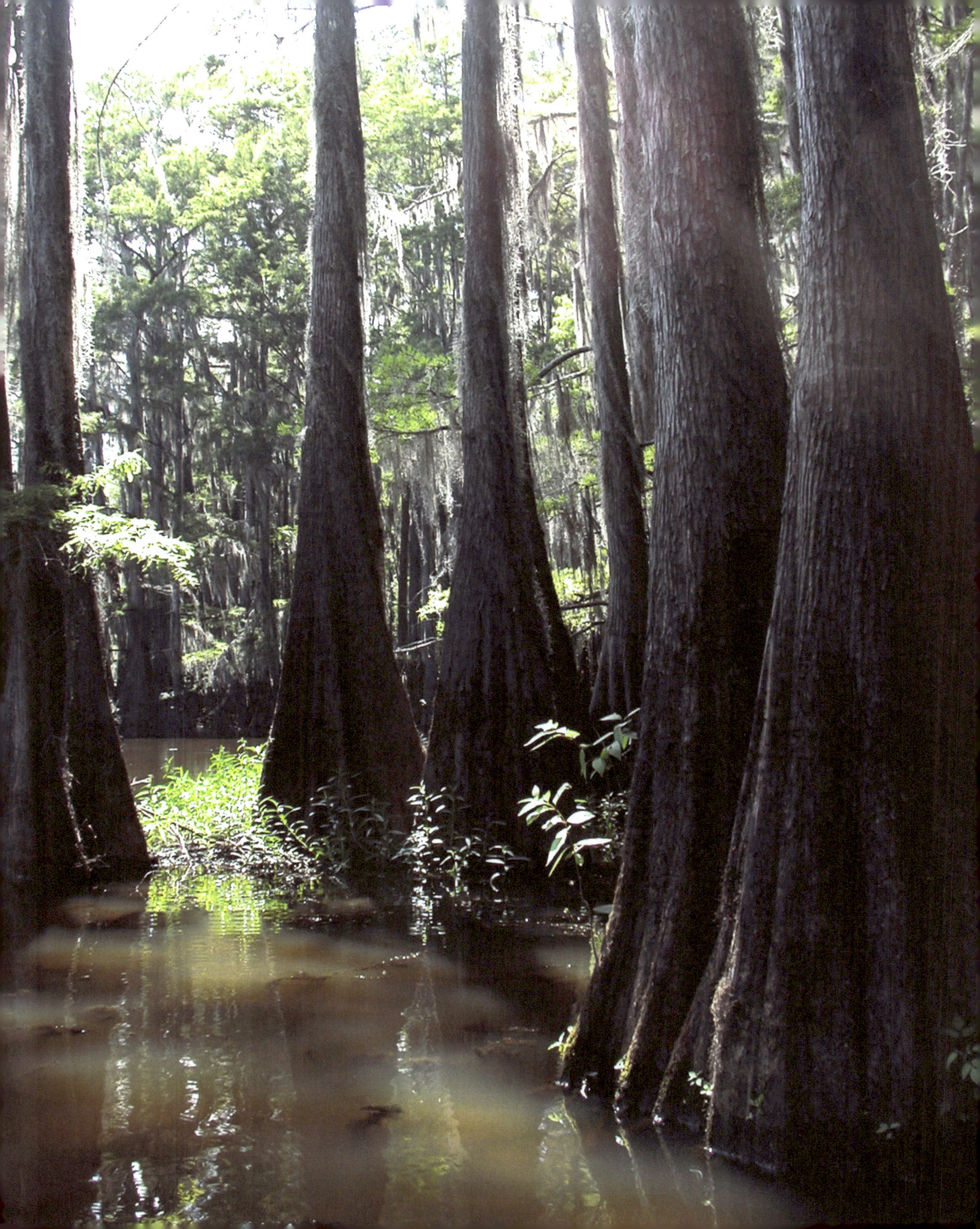

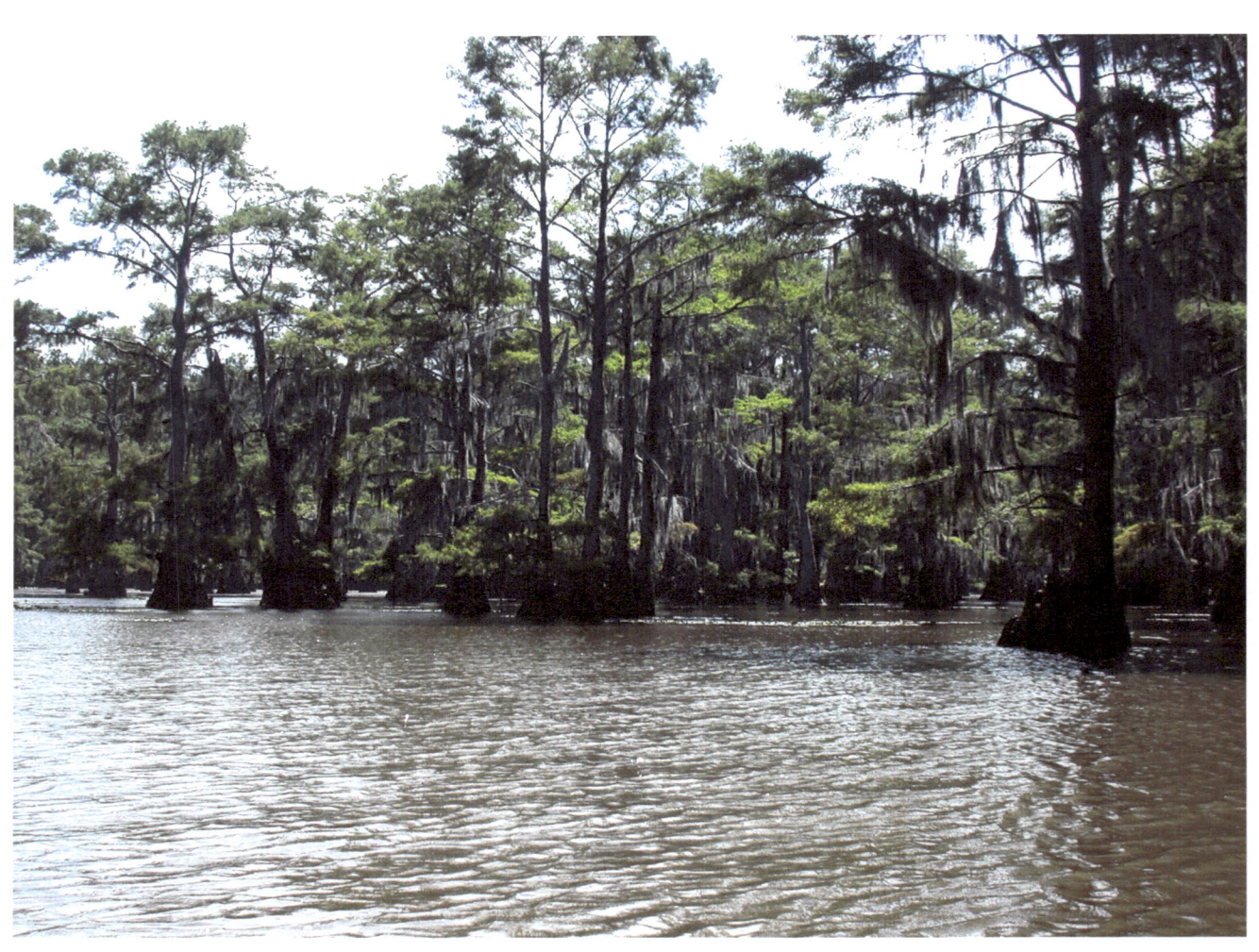

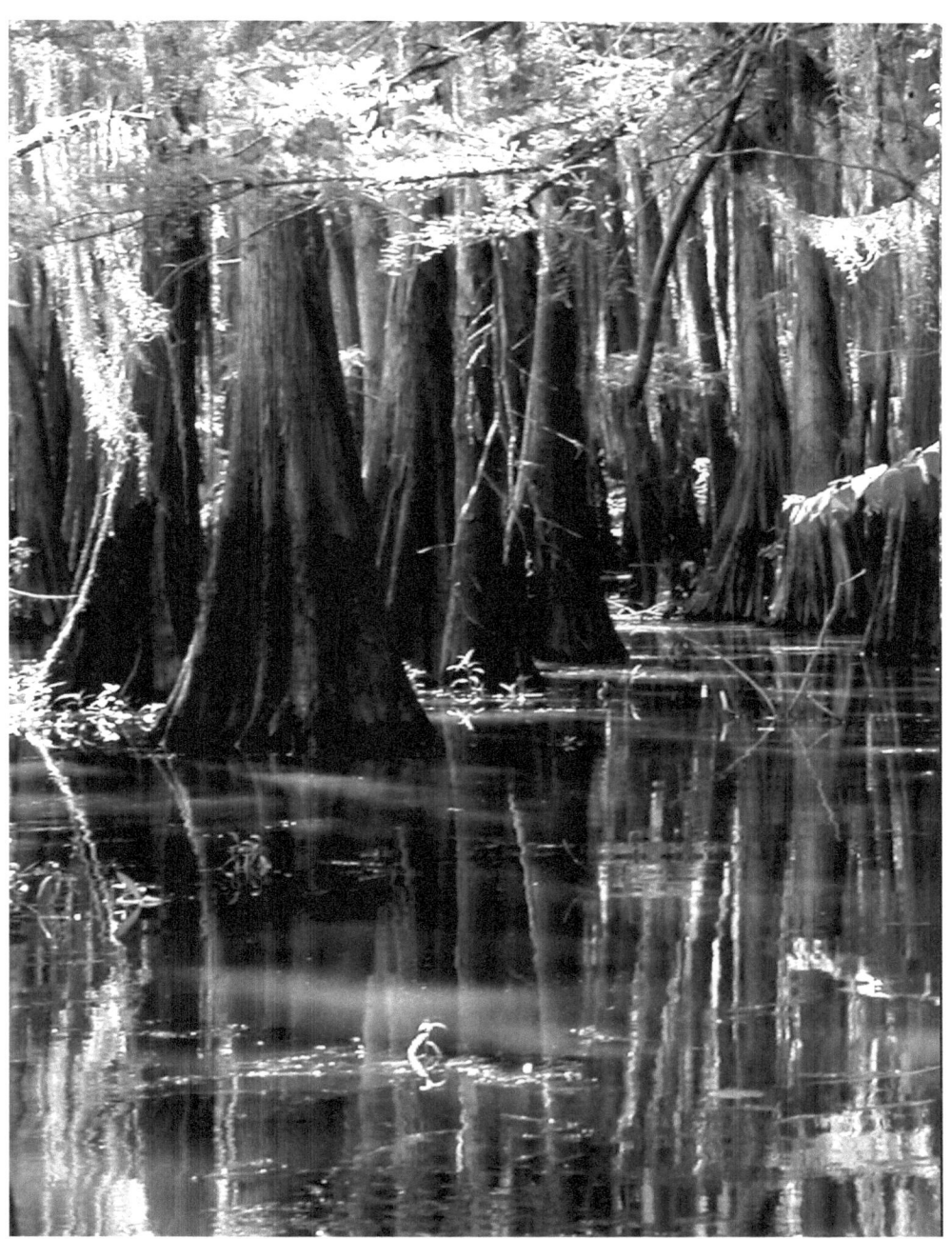

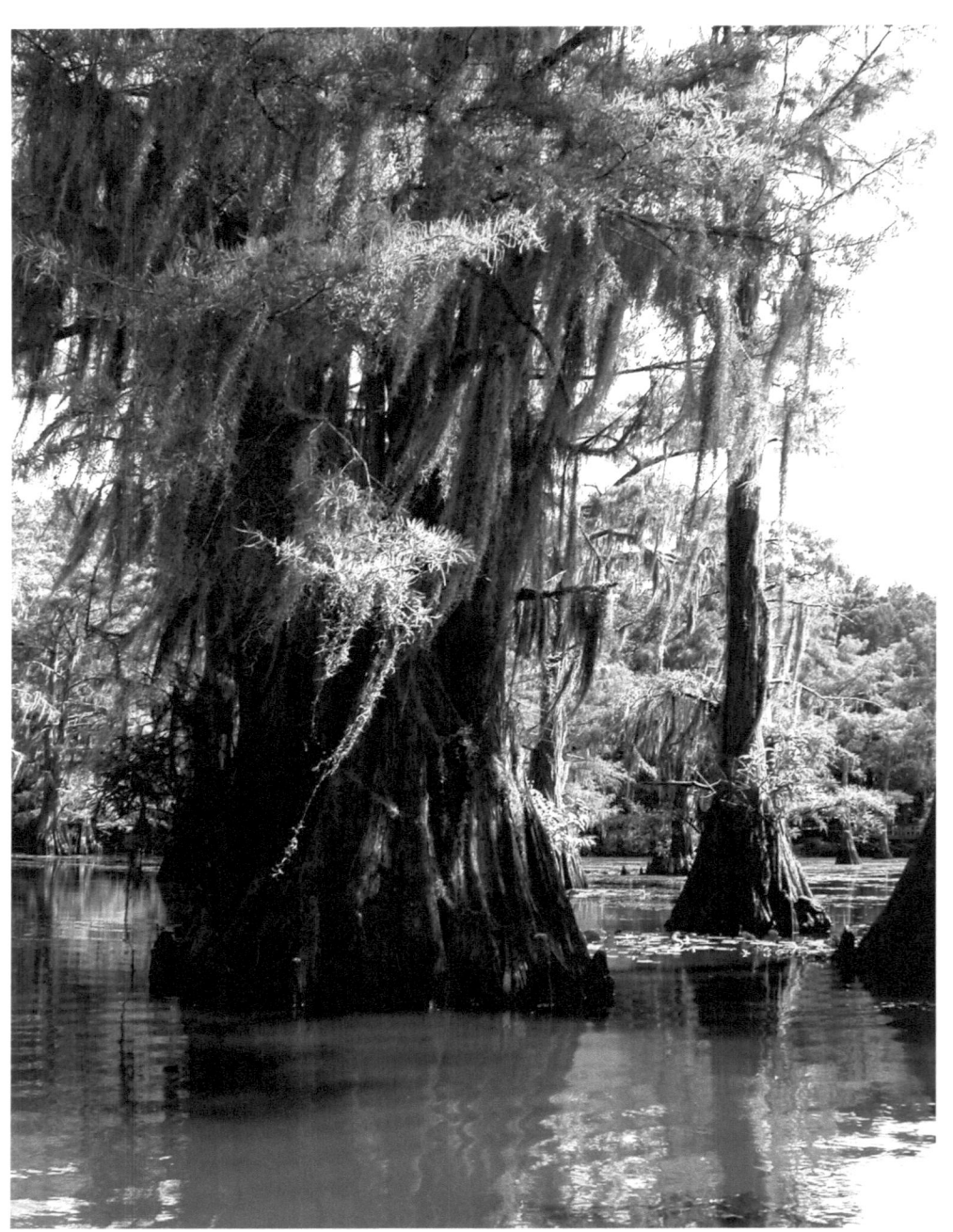

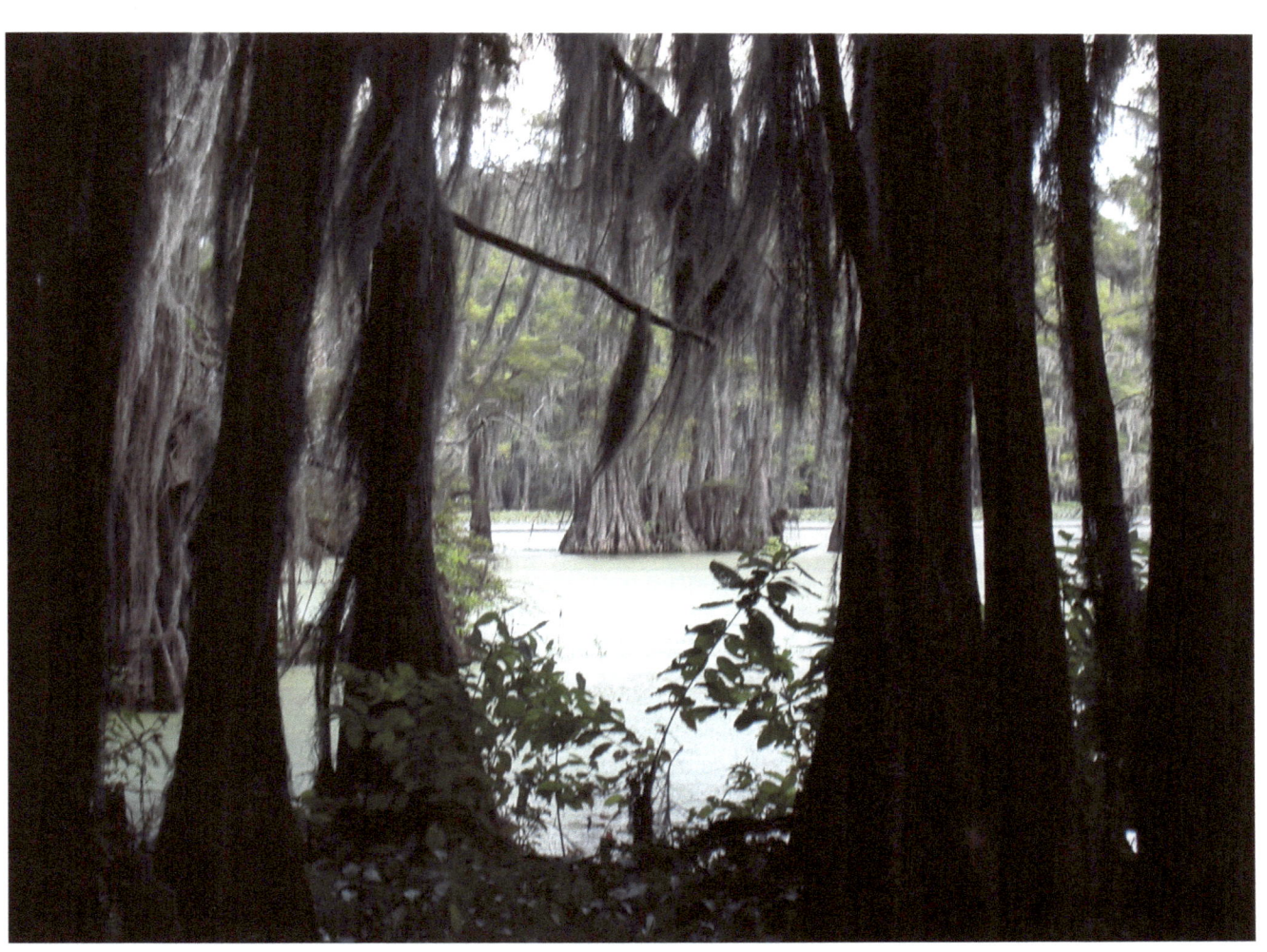

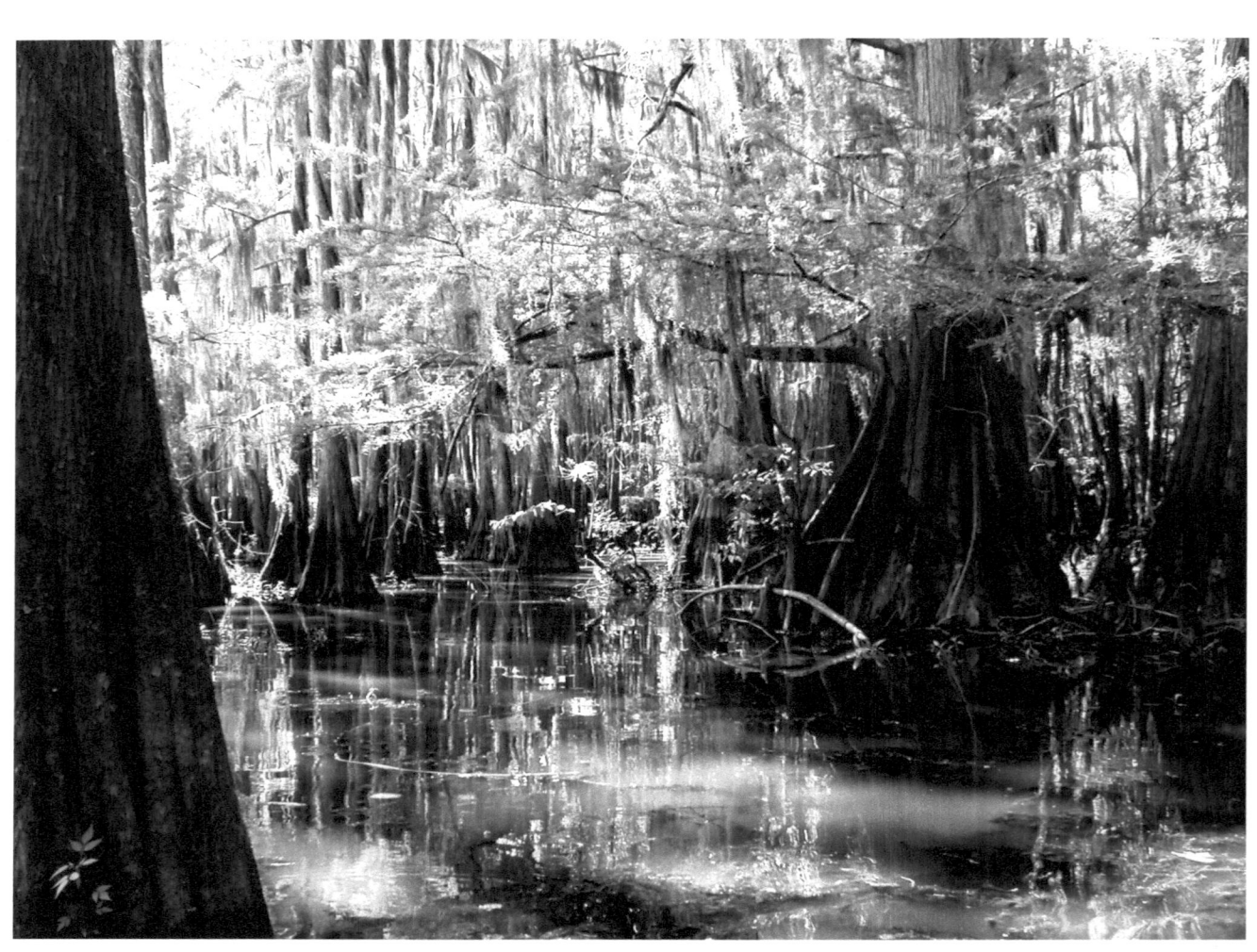

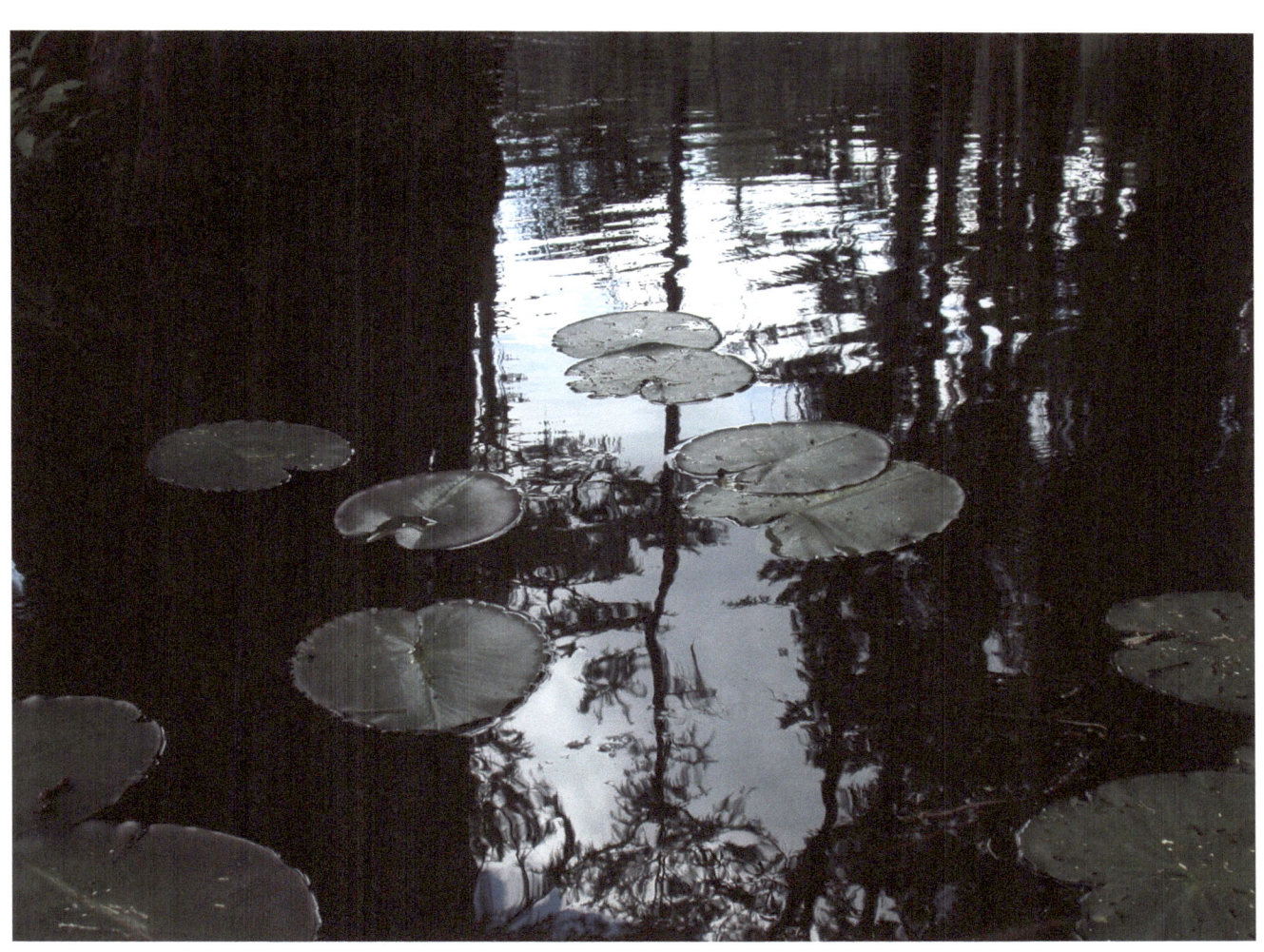

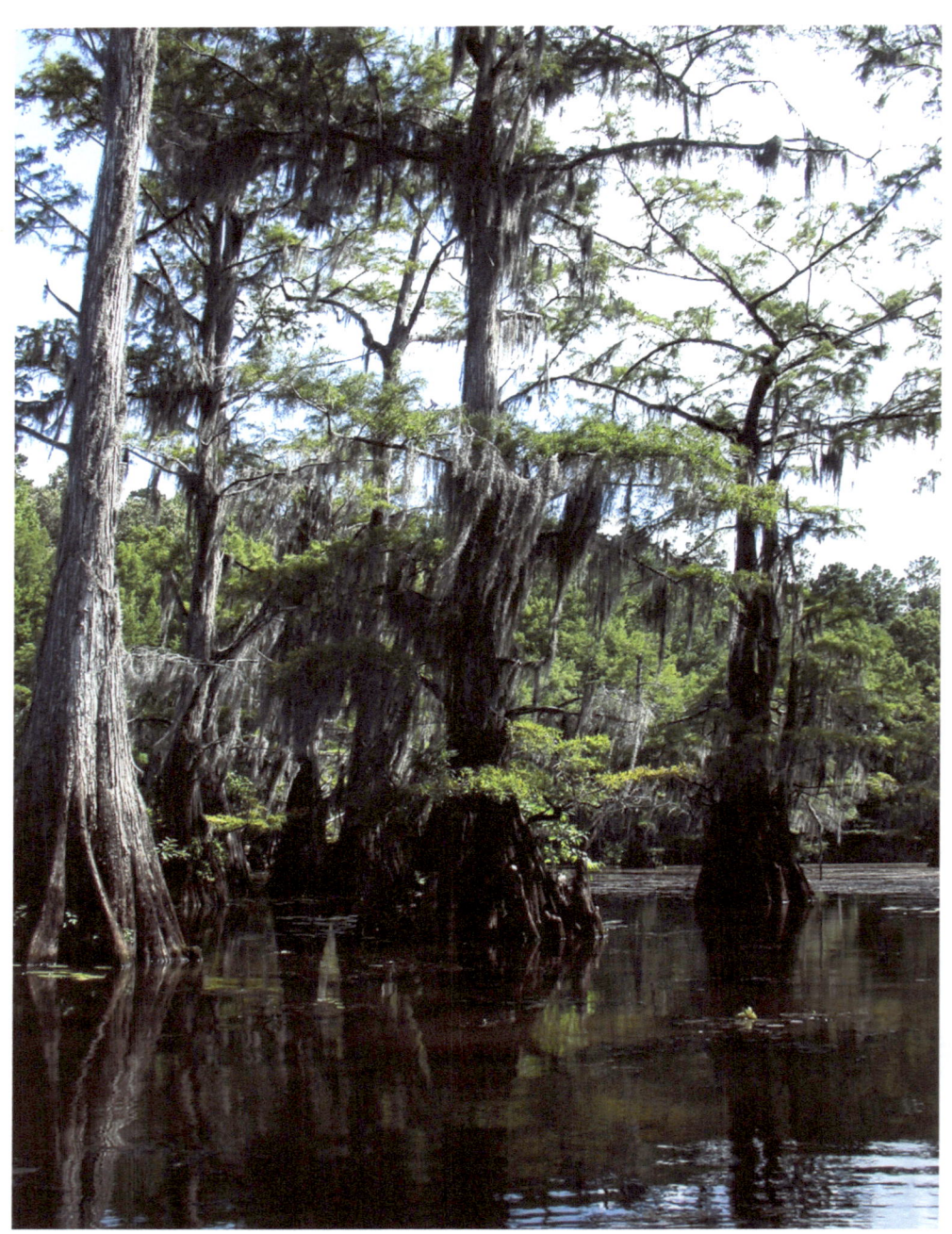

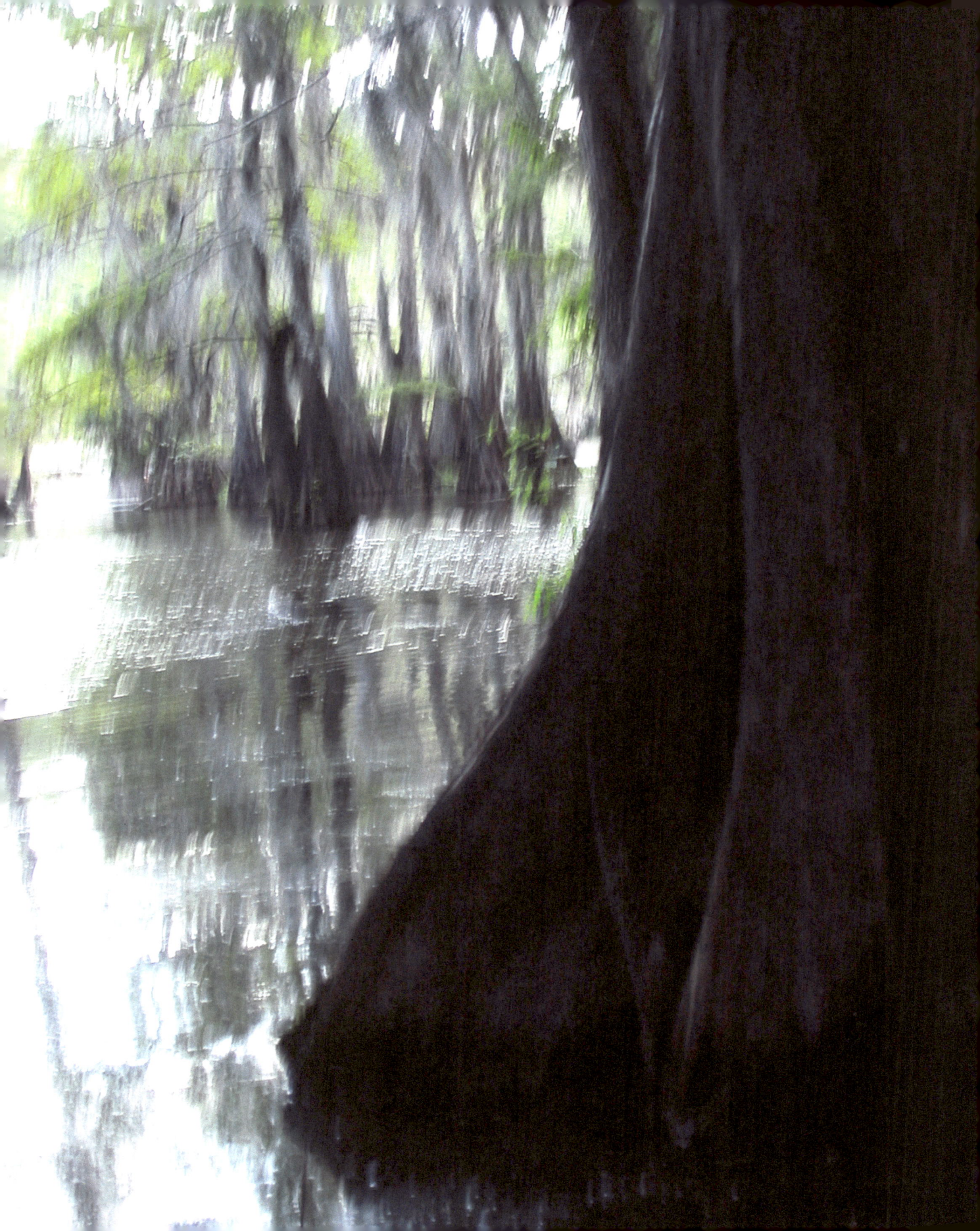

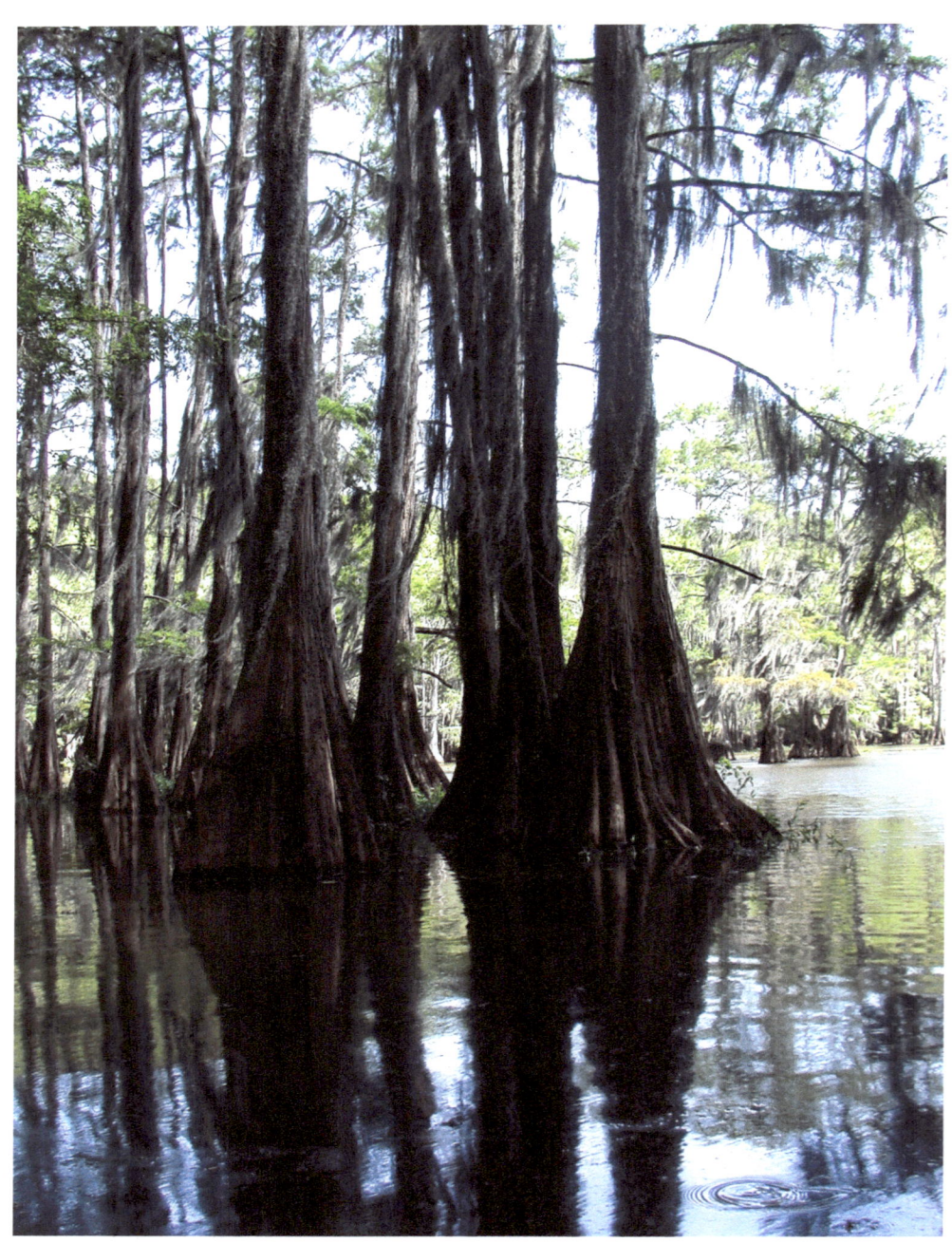

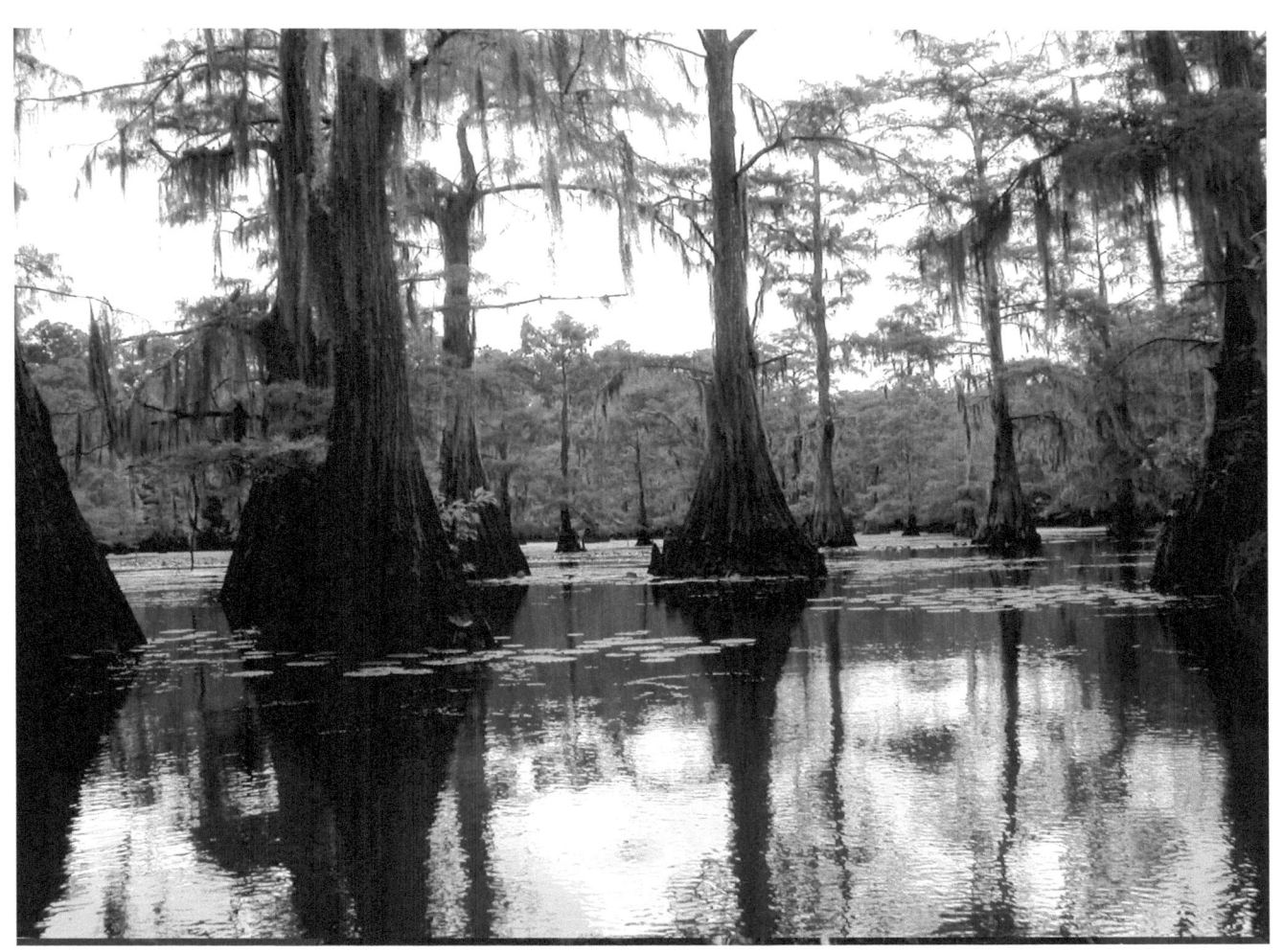

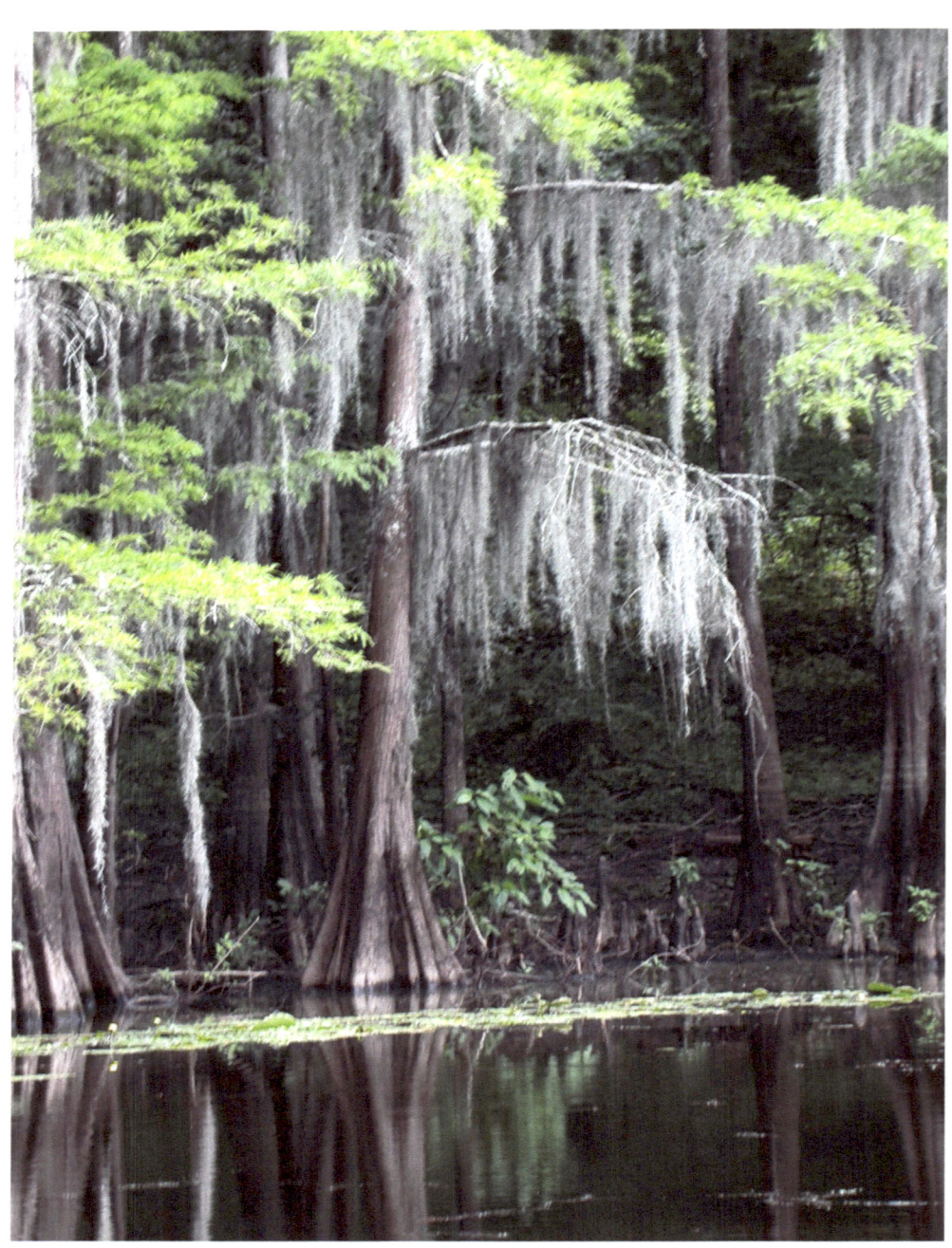

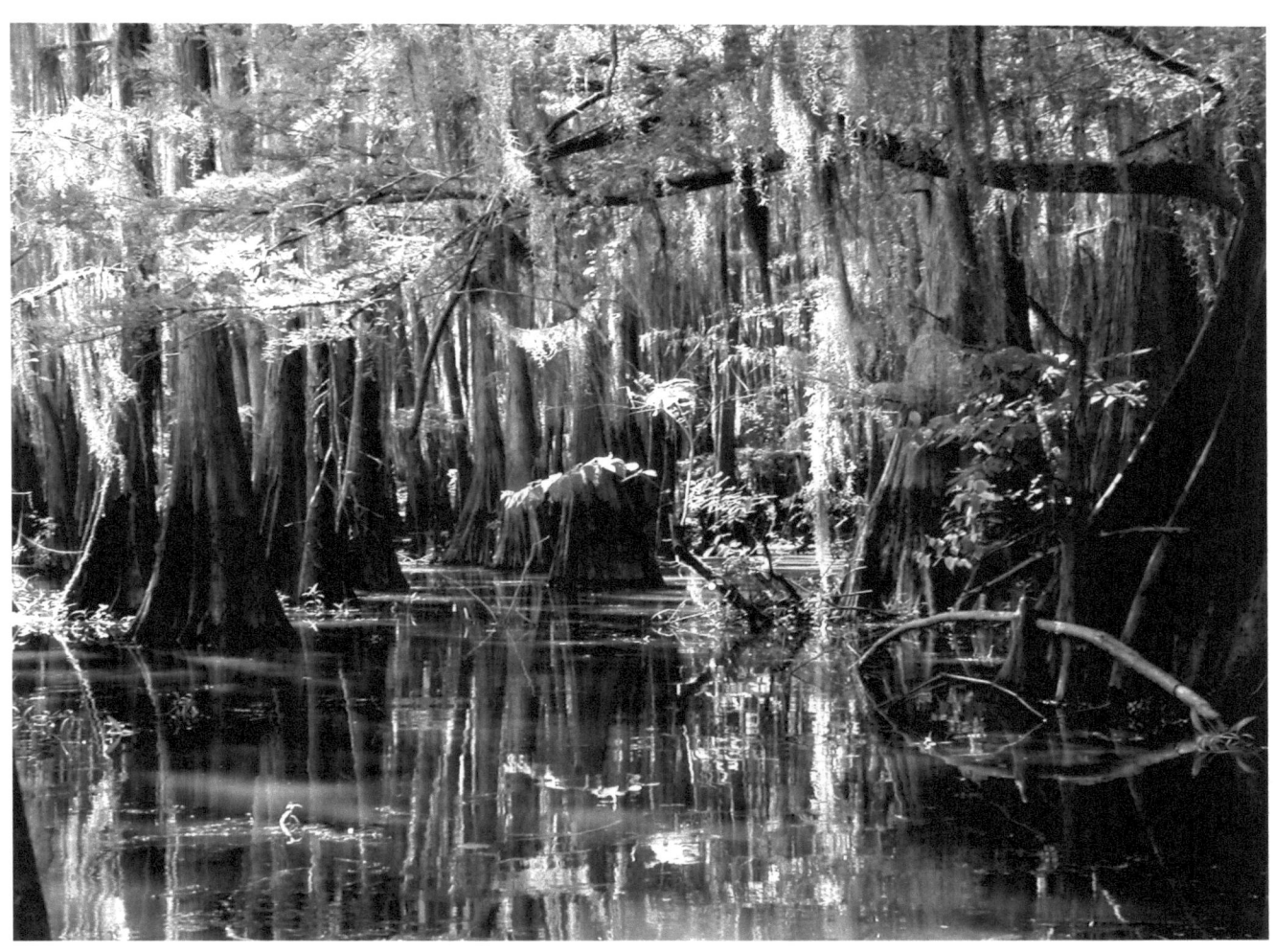

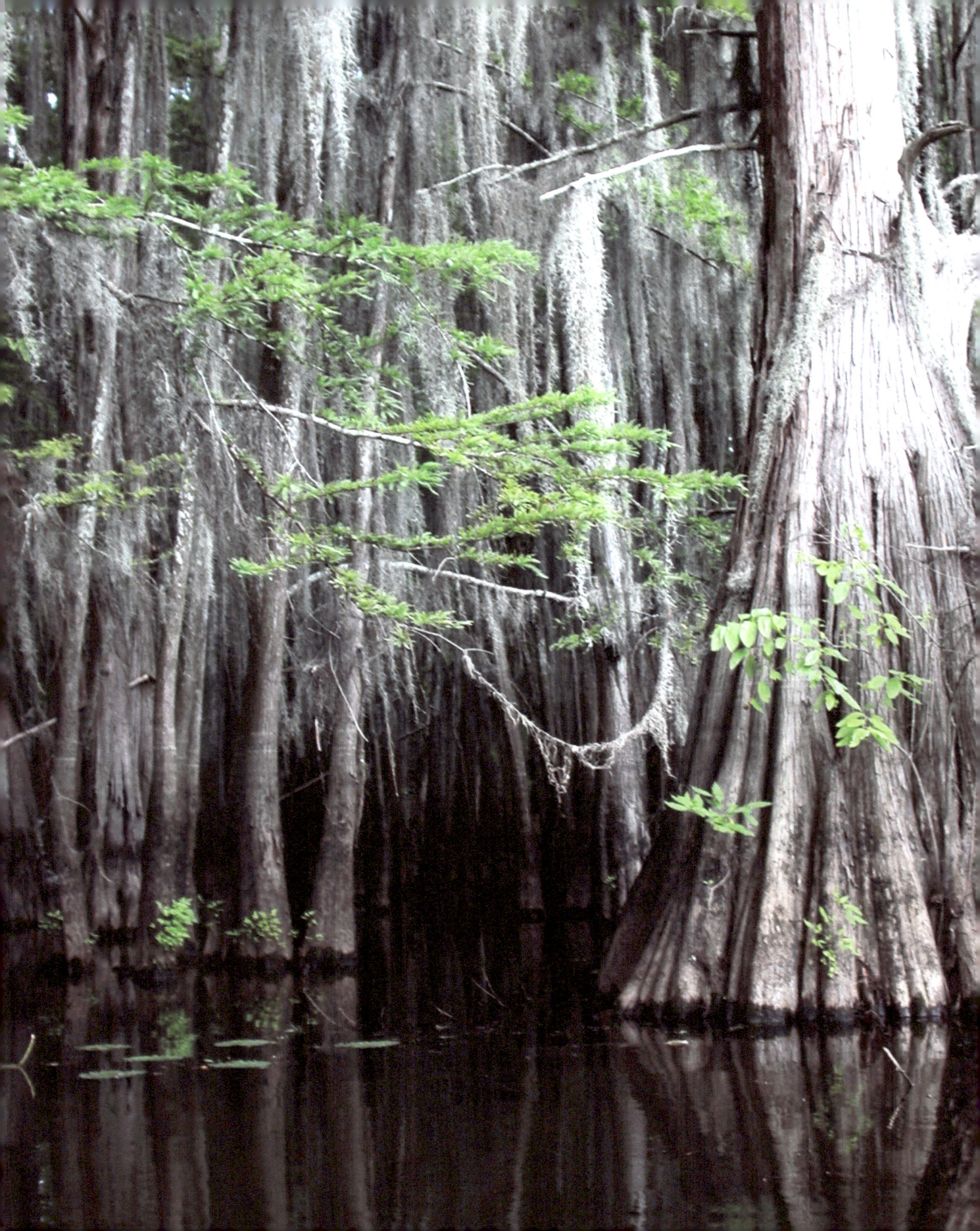

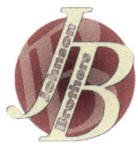